THE DIRTY DOZEN

PLUS ONE

CLAUDE R. TILLIS

References

How Did the Apostles Die? What We Actually Know

By Ryan Nelson | 17, 2019 | Bible characters

Seventy disciples

Wikipedia, the free encyclopedia

http://truthbook.com/jesus/the-twelve-apostles
http://christianity.about.com/od/peopleofthebible/tp/12-Apostles.htm

Truthbook.com denoted James "the Less" and Judas Thaddaeus as being twins.

(Acts 1:13) clearly denotes Judas as the brother of James, therefore, independent online research (other than truthbook.com) was performed on these two apostles.

Background Image by kjpargeter on Freepik

All images are copyright to their respective owners.

Waiver of Truth

All information comprised in this document (including the individual apostle documents) is not to be considered as being 100% accurate; however; all research work was performed with due diligence to be as accurate as possible.

Who Were the 12 Disciples and What Should We Know about Them?

Allyson Holland

Crosswalk.com Contributing Writer

Author's Disclaimer

I readily acknowledge that this book was created using references from existing writings. While other books exist with similar names and references, hopefully this book is different enough not to cause confusion OR infringement concerns.

Dedication

A Brief Background History About Pastor

Grandy

James W. Grandy, a native of Warren, Arkansas, moved to Los Angeles, California in the early '60s.

After serving two years in the United States Armed Forces, *(thank you for your service)* he was honorably discharged back into the civilian community. He worked and served continuously with the Los Angeles Rapid Transit District for over twenty-six years.

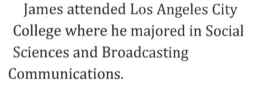

James attended Los Angeles City College where he majored in Social Sciences and Broadcasting Communications.

In 1973, he accepted his calling to the ministry and attended the *Los Angeles Bible Training School and Amity Community Bible School*, where he received his *Doctor of Divinity Degree* from Bradford University in 1978.

Seven years later, in 1985, he started an outreach ministry by organizing the **Christian Soul Clinic Church** of God in Christ, which he pastored until 1989 when he was called and appointed pastor of the **Bethany Church of God in Christ** located at 3916 South Budlong Avenue in Los Angeles, California. As he continued his studies, he received a *Master of Arts of Theology* on June 23, 2003, and the *Degree of Doctor of Theology* on September 16, 2005, both from North Carolina College of Theology.

Elder Grandy pastored Bethany with much prayer and great enthusiasm, especially praying that God would bless this little church in the middle of the neighborhood.

During his ministry at Bethany, his one burning desire was to mentor and raise up young men and women of God for future leadership in the church community. That dream was fulfilled after his passing when one of his ministers, Elder Tyrone Pearson, was elevated to Pastor and has prospered and served at Bethany to this date.

Contents

Preface

Greeting To All Friends Of The Gospel,

God has blessed me all the days of my life, from my birth and childhood to my current age of 72 years. Throughout the years, He brought many influential people into my life.

I have been in the ministry for over 40 years, serving in multiple capacities and roles on my journey as a minister of God. I served as the Assistant Pastor at my home church for most of those 40 years. After the passing of my pastor in 2015, I served as the interim pastor for two years and was elevated to the position of pastor in 2017.

On my Christian journey, God guided me to many men and women of the Gospel to direct me in the way I should go. Other than my pastor, one person who has deeply inspired and encouraged me as a believer, and later as a pastor, was Pastor James W. Grandy of the Bethany C.O.G.I.C. in Los Angeles, California.

In our travels together, we discussed many things. One night, as we traveled back from one of our Jurisdiction Convocation meetings, he mentioned that he was writing a book based on the calling of the 12 Apostles. He intended to title it "The Dirty Dozen." Unfortunately, we never delved into the details of how he planned to structure the book. Thus, this is my attempt to write it on his behalf. I hope you will recognize some familiar topics, but my aspiration is to present insights you might not have encountered before.

Join me as we delve into the lives and works of what Pastor Grandy termed "The Dirty Dozen." I've added a twist by including the phrase "Plus One." Hence, I invite you to enjoy what I've named "The Dirty Dozen, Plus One!"

Elder Claude R. Tillis, Jr

Pastor of Morning Star Church of God In Christ, Los Angeles, California- July, 2022

Introduction

Many of you have seen or at least have heard of the movie called *The Dirty Dozen.* This was a movie about a military operation during World War II, where a Major in the United States Army was given the assignment to organize a special group of men for a special task. He didn't choose men with the best record, nor did he choose the most athletic, the most intelligent, or the smartest men; however, he chose men who had the skill to get the job done. These men that were chosen were not the elite of the military, but they were more like the misfits of the army. By no stretch of the imagination were these men considered the cream of the crop or real leaders in any way. The same is true of the twelve men chosen by Christ to be the future leaders of the church. What I want you to know is that over two thousand years ago, there was another *Dirty Dozen,* and for clarity purposes, we can call them the *Original Dirty Dozen.*

At the beginning of His earthly ministry, Jesus called certain men to follow Him. His purpose was to teach them and introduce them to God Himself, to show them a more intimate way to interact with their God, to give them insight into how to allow God to lead their lives in the most victorious ways possible, and to reveal to them the power of God through the leadership of the Holy Spirit.

Although there were many disciples of Christ (the Bible numbers them at about 120), Jesus chose twelve men to spearhead and introduce his gospel message to the world. Their names are recorded in various places in scripture. For instance, let's look at Luke 6:12-16:

"And it came to pass in those days, that he went out into a mountain to pray and continued all night in prayer to God. When it was day, he called unto him his disciples: and of them he chose twelve, whom also he named apostles; Simon (whom he also named Peter), and Andrew his brother, James and John, Philip and Bartholomew, Thomas, James the son of Alphaeus, Simon called Zelotes, Judas the brother of James, and Judas Iscariot, who also was the traitor."

These are the twelve men chosen by Christ to be Apostles, and we have thus dubbed them *The Dirty Dozen.*

The title of this book is *The Dirty Dozen, Plus One.* We need to understand that it's not about the movie "The Dirty Dozen" but rather focuses on the initial twelve disciples, now called "Apostles." Men whom Jesus handpicked to be leaders in the church, spreading the *good news of the gospel* to the world.

2

The difference between this book and the movie lies in the title. The movie title is simply *The Dirty Dozen*, whereas the title of this book adds the phrase "plus one". What's that all about? The answer is this: We all know that among the initial twelve apostles, there was one who went astray, namely Judas Iscariot. After betraying Jesus, he took his own life (Matthew 27:3-5). The remaining apostles felt the need to replace Judas promptly before continuing the work Jesus had entrusted to them. So, they decided to hold an election to choose Judas's replacement.

Two men from the group of 120 disciples were nominated: Matthias and Joseph, also called Barsabbas or Justus. History records that Matthias was chosen to replace Judas Iscariot. However, Matthias is not the "plus one". That distinction belongs to Paul. After his encounter on the road to Damascus, during which he was blinded by the Lord and subsequently healed, Paul spent three years receiving private instruction from Jesus. Paul confirms his apostolic calling in places such as Romans 1:1 and Romans 1:5. This makes him the thirteenth Apostle or, as I refer to him in this book, "plus one".

Twelve men answered the call to be apostles of Christ. They were Jews, uneducated commoners, and men of simple

3

faith, who left everything behind to follow Christ. Jesus dedicated three years to preparing these men to become the future leaders of the church. His intention was for the apostles to eventually take over and continue the work He had initiated.

What we know to be true about Jesus is that He chose ordinary and unrefined men to be His disciples. They were the most common of the common. They hailed from the rural parts of the land, being farmers, carpenters, and fishermen — just plain folks from the area.

It's evident that Christ deliberately overlooked the elite, aristocratic, and influential men, choosing mostly from what some might call the dregs of society. That's consistent with God's way. He elevates the humble and lays low those who are proud. *"You didn't choose me. I chose you."* (John 14:16). Other scriptural passages that list the 12 Apostles can be found in the Gospel books of Matthew 10:2-4 and Mark 3:14-19.

Now that we're acquainted with the names of the apostles, let's delve deeper into the lives and stories of each of these men. So join me and meet *The Dirty Dozen, Plus One.*

But first, we need to clarify a few things, specifically, the difference between a "Disciple" and an "Apostle." Firstly, even today, ALL who follow Christ are "Disciples." However, within the community of Christ's followers, there's a hierarchy, with Apostles at the pinnacle. Regrettably, there's some ambiguity regarding who qualifies as an Apostle. Hopefully, the subsequent information will provide clarity on this matter.

We know that "Disciple" means a student and follower of Christ. In other words, throughout their time with Christ, from their calling to His ascension into heaven, they were disciples. The Greek word for disciples is "*mathetes*", which means "a learner, or a pupil." It could be said that they were disciplined to learn what was taught because the root of the word "disciple" is discipline.

Now, let's examine the word "Apostle" and its meaning.

The word "apostle" comes from the Greek word "*apostolos*", meaning "a delegate or messenger, one sent forth with orders". So, for the most part, apostles were disciples elevated to a higher level of responsibility in service to God. They were chosen and dispatched by God, specifically under the guidance of Christ before His ascension into heaven. Their mission or assignment was "to proclaim the gospel to the known world and to make disciples of all nations" (Matt 28:18-20; Acts 1:8).

To conclude, in addressing the controversy, I bring this up not to sow confusion but to hopefully provide clarity to a question long debated in the Christian community: "Who can be an apostle?" The only source from which we can derive this answer is scripture. The dictionary defines an "apostle" as "a delegate or messenger, one sent forth with orders".

Anyone who claims to be an apostle today must provide evidence for this as stated in Acts 1:21-22. Here is what God says, *"So one of the men who have accompanied us during all the time that the Lord Jesus went in and out among us, beginning from the baptism of John until the day when he was taken up from us—one of these men must become with us a witness to his resurrection."*

Notice that the qualifications for being an apostle are laid out in Scripture and should not be set by the will or beliefs of men.

As we see, the scripture states that an apostle should be "men who have accompanied Jesus during all the time that the Lord went in and out among them." They must also be an "eyewitness to his resurrection."

But wait, there's more; they must have been with Jesus

from the beginning of his ministry, that is, from "the baptism of John until the day when Jesus was taken up into heaven."

You see, the word "MUST" is a conditional statement. Any apostle MUST have been with the Lord from the day that Jesus was baptized until the time he was taken into heaven, and they MUST have also been with the disciples and had been "a witness to his resurrection" (Acts 1:22). That excludes 100% of all of us today and everyone in the recent past because no one is over 2,000 years old. Therefore, anyone who claims to be an apostle today is gravely mistaken and, biblically speaking, cannot even qualify as one.

To recap, we now know that the word "Disciple" means a student and follower of Christ. We also understand that an "Apostle" is one who was personally chosen and called by Jesus, then sent out to proclaim the gospel and make disciples throughout the world.

Of course, Jesus had more than 12 disciples or followers. In fact, Acts 1:15-26 tells us Jesus had at least 120 disciples or followers. *"And in those days Peter stood up in the midst of the disciples, and said, (the number of names together was about a hundred and twenty,)"*.

It's important to recognize that Jesus had more than 12 disciples or followers. However, Luke explains that Jesus elevated some of them to the office of "Apostle". *"One day soon afterward Jesus went up on a mountain to pray, and he prayed to God all night. At daybreak, he called together all of his disciples and chose twelve of them to be apostles. Here are their names: Simon (whom he named Peter), Andrew (Peter's brother), James, John, Philip, Bartholomew, Matthew, Thomas, James (son of Alphaeus), Simon (who was called the zealot), Judas (son of James), Judas Iscariot (who later betrayed him)."* (Luke 6:12-16 NLT)

Now, let's delve into the lives of these *Dirty Dozen, Plus One* and see what insights we can gather from their lives. To make this book more engaging, I've decided to present the apostles in the format of men wanted by the government. After the crucifixion of Jesus, His followers essentially became fugitives. In my imagination, these men were viewed as criminals and pursued by the authorities. Therefore, I'm presenting them with their details framed as a police "Rap Sheet". Enjoy...

OFFICIAL

RAP

SHEETS

PETER AND ANDREW

And He said to them, "Follow Me, and I will make you fishers of men."

- Matthew 4:19

Peter and Andrew, whose father was John, were born in Bethsaida. Later, they lived in Capernaum. They were fishermen by trade and worked alongside the sons of Zebedee, James, and John.

Peter and Andrew started out as disciples of John the Baptist. It was Andrew who introduced his older brother Peter to Jesus while on a journey in the wilderness with John the Baptist (John 1:40-42). After Peter was introduced to Jesus, both he and Andrew became followers of Jesus.

PETER

IMPRISONED REPEATEDLY IN JERUSALEM
WITH HIS WIFE

EVANGELIZED BABYLON (WROTE 1 PETER))

LATER IN ROME, TEAMED UP WITH JOHN
MARK

TORTURED NINE MONTHS, THEN HE WAS
CRUCIFIED

Rap Sheet

Peter

AKA Simon, Simon Peter, or Cephas (the Rock)

Jesus said unto him, Verily I say unto thee, That this night, before the cock crow, thou shalt deny me thrice.

- Matthew 26:34

Peter was the one who tended to associate with others of his own kind. He was a natural leader, which made him the obvious spokesperson for the other disciples. He is mentioned more times in the gospels than any other disciple. He was the older brother of Andrew. (Luke 4:38) His wife often traveled with him on his missionary journeys (1 Cor. 9:5).

His assignment was to bring the Gospel to the circumcised; in other words, his mission was to preach to the Jews (Gal. 2:7). Without a doubt, Peter is the disciple most people can relate to. One minute he is walking on water by faith with Jesus, and the next, he is sinking in doubt, like denying three times that he even knew Jesus. He was impulsive and emotional. Despite all of his faults, he was dearly loved by Christ.

After His crucifixion and resurrection, and shortly before Jesus ascended into heaven, He had one more blessing for Peter: restoration. Jesus restored Peter back to his leadership position by asking Peter a seemingly simple question three times. While we know Peter for walking on water with Jesus, he is better known for denying Christ three times after Jesus was arrested by the high priest's guards. However, thanks be to God, Jesus knew Peter's heart. He asked Peter three times, "Do you love me?" Peter's response each time was, "Yes, I do." And Jesus' response each time was, "Feed my sheep." This was a statement of restoration, that brought Peter back to his place of leadership among the other Apostles.

After the death of Jesus and His ascension into heaven, Peter became an even bolder and more outspoken evangelist and missionary for the Gospel, and eventually, one of the greatest leaders of the early church.

Historians have recorded that when Peter was sentenced to crucifixion, he did not feel worthy to die the same way his Savior died, so he

requested to be crucified upside down. He died a martyr's death in Rome during the reign of Nero.

(**Quick note:** It is believed that Paul was beheaded about the same time Peter was crucified)

ANDREW

EVANGELIZED ALONG THE CAUCASUS
MOUNTAINS AND CASPIAN SEA IN EASTER
EUROPE

PREACHED IN ISTANBUL AND LATER ON TO
MACEDONIA AND GREECE

HUNG FROM A CROSS IN GREECE FOR THREE
DAYS, PREACHING THE LOVE OF JESUS TO HIS
PERSECUTORS

Rap Sheet

Andrew

Andrew was a disciple of John the Baptist. One day, as John the Baptist, Andrew, and John, the son of Zebedee, were together, they saw Jesus coming down the road. When John the Baptist recognized who He was, he said, "*Behold, the Lamb of God!*"(John 1:35)

After spending a short time with Jesus, Andrew abandoned John the Baptist and became the first follower or disciple of this Jesus of Nazareth. This didn't bother John because he knew his mission was to point people to the Messiah, and that's exactly what he did.

Andrew was the first one to join Jesus as a disciple. His enthusiasm was evident; the Bible says, "*The first thing*

Andrew did was to find his brother Simon and tell him, 'We have found the Messiah' (that is, the Christ)." His first thought was to introduce his older brother, Peter, to Jesus. This desire revealed a deep love for God already burning in his heart.

Although Andrew led Peter to Christ, he unselfishly stepped into the background and allowed his more boisterous brother to become one of the powerful leaders of the group and of the church. Even though Andrew was not a dominant personality like his older, outspoken brother, he was an emotional and passionate preacher, proclaiming the gospel with boldness.

The Gospels don't tell us a great deal about Andrew, but reading between the lines reveals a person who thirsted for truth and found it in the living water of Jesus Christ. In Andrew's life, we see how one day a simple fisherman dropped his nets on the shore and went on to become an amazing fisher of men.

Andrew faced crucifixion with boldness and courage, dying a martyr's death. He said these words: *"Oh, cross most welcome and longed for! With a willing mind, joyfully and desirously, I come to you, being a scholar of Him who hung on you. I have always been your lover and yearn to embrace you."*

According to tradition, Andrew was martyred by crucifixion in the Greek city of Patras around 60 AD. Like his brother Peter, Andrew didn't consider himself worthy to die in the same way as Jesus. Thus, he was bound—not nailed—to a cross that was hung in an "X" shape instead of a "T" shape. For this reason, an X-shaped cross is sometimes referred to as Saint Andrew's Cross.

"And Jesus, walking by the sea of Galilee, saw two brethren, Simon called Peter, and Andrew his brother, casting a net into the sea: for they were fishers. And he saith unto them, Follow me, and I will make you fishers of men."

- Matthew 4: 18 -19

JAMES & JOHN
SONS OF ZEBEDEE

History indicates that there is some evidence that Mr. Zebedee was a man of affluence and wealth. He owned his own business and was the owner and CEO of what we'll call **"the Zebedee Fishing Company"**. Mr. Zebedee was able to hire enough men to help with his fishing business. (Mark 1:20).

Even though James is listed before his younger brother John in scripture, little is truly known about him other than the fact that he is part of what we call **"Jesus' inner circle"**. John seems to be more in the forefront of what is happening during the three-year ministry of Christ. James and John were both men of intense passion and zeal for the gospel. Given their enthusiasm, Jesus nicknamed them **"the Sons of Thunder"**. (Mark 3:17)

JAMES

Brother of John the Beloved and son of Salome (Mary's sister)

Was first to be martyred

Lived 14 years after Jesus's death

Preached the Gospel throughout Spain

Beheaded by Herod Agrippa in Jerusalem on Easter 44 AD

Rap Sheet

James

James, the elder brother of John, appears to be the quieter of the disciples, as we don't read much about him in Scripture. Each of the gospels identifies James as an early disciple of Christ. James, the son of Zebedee, was often called James the Greater to distinguish him from the other disciple named James.

As part of Jesus' **"inner circle,"** alongside his brother John and their friend Peter, he was present when Jesus raised Jairus' daughter from the dead (Mark 5:37).

He was also a witness to Jesus' transfiguration on the Mount of Olives (Matthew 17:1). He was with Jesus in the Garden of Gethsemane just before Jesus was arrested. There,

James heard Jesus ask God to let the cup of crucifixion pass Him by and also heard Jesus say, *"but nevertheless, let your will be done"* (Mark 14:33).

Both James and John were so passionate about the word of God that they earned a special nickname from the Lord: "sons of thunder."

James was the first apostle to be martyred for his faith. In A.D. 44, he was beheaded, making him one of only two apostles (along with Judas Iscariot) whose martyrdom is recorded in Scripture. He was executed with a sword. *"It was about this time that King Herod arrested some who belonged to the church, intending to persecute them. He had James, the brother of John, put to death with the sword"* (Acts 12:1-2).

King Herod aimed to win the favor of the Jews. Since the Jewish leadership was intent on preventing Christianity from spreading, Herod believed that persecuting Christians would please his Jewish subjects—and it did (Acts 12:3).

James, son of Zebedee, and his brother John were named by

Jesus as Boanerges, which means "sons of thunder"

Mark 3:17

JOHN
THE BELOVED

Brother of James and son of Salome
(Mary's sister)

Moved to Ephesus just before 70AD
perhaps with Aunt Mary

Exiled to Patmos (Wrote Revelations)

Died Last, 68 years after his Lord

"Little children, love one another."

Rap Sheet

John

AKA the Beloved

John, along with his brother James, was nicknamed by Jesus as the **"sons of thunder."** However, John, for obvious reasons, preferred to be known as the "disciple whom Jesus loved."

Due to his fierce temperament and special devotion to Christ, John earned a special place in Christ's **"inner circle,"** which included his brother James and Peter (John 3:23).

John wrote a significant portion of the New Testament. He penned the Gospel of John, 1 John, 2 John, 3 John, and the book of Revelation. Seemingly impressed by the love Jesus held for the church, John wrote more about love than any other gospel writer. Due to his close relationship with Jesus, John received firsthand knowledge about God's love for humanity and about mutual human affection.

John was exiled to the island of Patmos during the reign of Caesar Domitian. However, after Domitian's death, John was permitted to return to Ephesus, where he oversaw churches in Asia until his death around A.D. 100.

John's dynamic personality had a profound impact on the early church. In his writings, he was unafraid to highlight contrasting characteristics. For example, on the first Easter (Christ's resurrection), Scripture depicts John racing Peter to the tomb after Mary Magdalene announced it was empty. Although John reached the tomb first, he graciously stepped aside, allowing Peter to enter before him (John 20:1-9).

Before Jesus died, He entrusted His mother, Mary, to John the Beloved (John 19:26–27). After Mary's death, John moved to Ephesus, where he wrote his three epistles. He was exiled to the island of Patmos by Caesar Domitian for preaching the Gospel. It was there that he received a revelation from Christ and penned the Book of Revelation. After Caesar Domitian's death, John returned to Ephesus, where he oversaw churches and lived out the remaining years of his life. He died a natural death at the age of 94, around 100 AD.

Traditionally, John is regarded as the only apostle to die of old age. While some accounts suggest a few other apostles might have died of natural causes, John's death is traditionally the most well-documented.

"And going on from thence, he saw other two brethren, James the son of Zebedee, and John his brother, in a ship with Zebedee their father, mending their nets; and he called them. "And they immediately left the ship and their father, and followed him".

- Matthew 4:22-23

PHILIP

AFTER THE ASCENSION, PHILIP TRAVELED TO
SOUTH RUSSIA AND PREACHED 20 YEARS

JOINED BARTHOLOMEW TO PREACH IN
LAODICEA, COLOSSE, AND HIEROPOLIS

HEALED AND CONVERTED PROCONSUL'S WIFE

PROCONSUL CRUCIFIED HIM AT THE AGE OF 87

Rap Sheet

Phillip

"The next day He purposed to go into Galilee, and He found Philip. And Jesus said to him, Follow Me."

- John 1:43

We don't know a lot about Philip's past. We know he was a Jew, even though he was known by his Greek name, Philip. We know he had a heart for evangelism because he was anxious to tell his friend Nathanael that the One foretold by Moses and the prophets had been found.

"Philip found Nathanael and said to him, "We have found him of whom Moses in the Law and also the prophets wrote, Jesus of Nazareth the son of Joseph."

- John 1:45

Philip and Nathanael were close companions and may have studied the Old Testament together. We also know that he was one of the first followers of Jesus Christ. John records more about Philip than any other in the Gospel. It was Philip who ask Jesus, *"Lord, show us the Father, and we will be satisfied." Jesus replies, "Have I been with you all this time, Philip, and yet you still don't know who I am? Anyone who has seen me has seen the Father!"* (NLT) (John 14:8–9)

History shows that Christians have confused Philip the Apostle with Philip the Evangelist from the Book of Acts. Philip the Evangelist is the Philip that was a deacon in the history of the early church in the book of Acts.

After the ascension of Christ, it is believed that Apostle Philip preached the gospel in Asia Minor at Phrygia. There are conflicting stories about how Philip died. Some say he was beheaded; some say he was stoned to death. Others say he was crucified upside down.

However, what we do know is that he died sometime in the first century, possibly around 80 AD. Most of the earliest traditions seem to point to him being martyred in the ancient Greek city of Hierapolis. Polycrates of Ephesus wrote in a letter to Pope Victor, *"I speak of Philip, one of the twelve apostles, who is laid to rest at Hierapolis. . ."*

NATHANEAL

OR BARTHOLOMEW

Prayed 100x each day and 100x each
night

Voice like a trumpet, knew many
languages, always cheerful

Ordered to be crucified with Philip but
taken down

Preached in Armenia with Jude

Flayed (skin peeled off) alive in
Azerbaijan in 68 AD

Rap Sheet

Nathaneal

Nathanael means "God has given" in Hebrew. Interestingly, only the Gospel of John uses the name Nathanael; the other three gospels refer to him as "Bartholomew."

He hailed from Cana in Galilee (John 21:2). For some unknown reason, he expressed prejudice against the city of Nazareth. After Jesus went to Galilee and found Philip, the Bible tells us that *Philip found Nathanael and said to him, "We have found the one Moses wrote about in the Law, and about whom the prophets also wrote—Jesus of Nazareth, the son of Joseph"* (John 1:45). In conversation with Philip, Nathanael expressed his skepticism, asking, *"Can anything good come out of Nazareth?"* (John 1:46).

Such disbelief was understandable since Nazareth was an obscure, remote hill town of little consequence. It lacked sophistication and glamour, quite the opposite of what one might expect. It wasn't a place where many would anticipate the Messiah's origins. However, despite his skepticism, Nathanael followed Philip to meet Jesus.

When Jesus saw Nathanael coming toward Him, He said, *"Here truly is an Israelite in whom there is no deceit"* (John 1:47). Nathanael wondered how Jesus knew his character, because they had never met. Jesus continued and said, *"I saw you while you were still under the fig tree before Philip called you"* (John 1:48). Nathanael then immediately recognized Jesus as the Messiah, calling him the *"Son of God"* and the *"King of Israel"* (John 1:49).

While scripture doesn't provide extensive details about Nathanael, he became a faithful follower of Jesus Christ. Historical accounts suggest he might have preached in India and translated the book of Matthew into the local language.

Nathanael met martyrdom while serving the people of Albinopolis, Armenia. He was likely flayed (his skin peeled from his body) and then beheaded.

MATTHEW

ALSO CALLED LEVI, BROTHER OF JAMES (SON OF ALPHAEUS)

REMAINED IN JERUSALEM FOR 15 YEARS BEFORE HIS MISSIONARY JOURNEYS

PREACHED IN PERSIA, ETHIOPIA, AND EGYPT

MARTYRED IN EGYPT

Rap Sheet

Matthew

AKA Levi

"As Jesus went on from there, He saw a man called Matthew, sitting in the tax collector's booth; and He said to him, Follow Me! And he got up and followed Him. "

- Matthew 9:9

Matthew, the son of Alphaeus, was a tax collector or a Customs Official for Rome in the city of Capernaum. Even though Mathew was a Jew, the Jews hated him because he worked for Rome and betrayed his own people. Because they abused their power, tax collectors were among the most despised people in all of Israel. They were known for over-taxing the people to line their own pockets.

"Then it happened that as Jesus was reclining at the table in the house, behold, many tax collectors and sinners came and were dining with Jesus and His disciples; for there were many of them, and they were following Him. When the scribes of the Pharisees saw that He was eating with the sinners and tax collectors, they said to His disciples, Why is he eating and drinking with tax collectors and sinners? And hearing this, Jesus said to them, It is not those who are healthy that need a physician, but those who are sick; I did not come to call the righteous, but sinners."

- Mark 2:16

Upon hearing those simple words from Jesus, "Follow me," Matthew, the once-dishonest tax collector, abandoned everything and obeyed. Just like us, he yearned for acceptance and love. Recognizing Jesus as a figure worthy of sacrifice, Matthew willingly relinquished his comfortable existence to serve and accompany Christ.

Matthew took the gospel to Ethiopia and Egypt. Unfortunately, around 60 AD, King Hyrcanus had him executed with a halberd—a spear affixed with an ax—in the city of Nadabah, Ethiopia.

THOMAS

COMMONLY KNOWN AS "DOUBTING THOMAS"

ESTABLISHED THE CHRISTIAN CHURCH IN
BABYLON AS A FEARLESS EVANGELIST AND
GREAT CHURCH BUILDER

MOVED ON TO PREACH IN PERSIA (IRAN), THEN
TO INDIA. PREACHED AS FAR AS CHINA.

KILLED WITH A LANCE NEAR CHENNAI IN
49 AD

Rap Sheet

Thomas

Aka Didymus, meaning the Twin, although a twin brother or sister is never mentioned in the Bible

Thomas, also known as Didymus, which means "The Twin" (even though a twin sibling is never mentioned in scripture), is historically remembered as "Doubting Thomas" due to his initial refusal to believe in Jesus' resurrection until he saw and touched Christ's physical body himself. In the context of disciples' actions, history seems to have unfairly judged Thomas. After all, with the exception of John, each of the 12 disciples abandoned Jesus during His trial and on the cross.

Thomas was a vocal skeptic and could be considered a pessimist. The first three gospels don't offer much detail about Thomas; they simply mention his name.

In John 11:16, Thomas is first mentioned when Lazarus dies and the disciples are concerned for their safety if they return to Bethany. In a remarkably bold statement, Thomas speaks up and says, "*Let us also go, that we may die with Him*" (John 11:16). This instance reveals qualities not often attributed to Thomas—qualities of courage and loyalty to Christ.

That same devotion to Christ becomes evident when Jesus announced to the disciples that He was going away to prepare a place for them. We hear Thomas's response when Jesus said, *"'And you know the way where I am going.' Thomas said to Him, 'Lord, we do not know where you are going, how do we know the way?'"* (John 14:4-5) Thomas sought clarity from Jesus because he was determined not to be left behind.

It appears that Thomas had a tendency toward extremes. Earlier, he had displayed courageous faith, showing his willingness to risk his life to follow Jesus anywhere, even unto death. There's an important lesson to learn from Thomas's life: If we genuinely seek the truth and are open about our struggles and doubts with ourselves and others, God will faithfully reveal Himself to us, just as He did for Thomas. This is the true reason we hear Thomas exclaim, *"My Lord and My God!"* (John 20:28)

Tradition strongly suggests that Thomas established a church in India, where he is believed to have been martyred in Mylapore, India, in 72 AD. He was killed with a spear.

"Now Thomas (also known as Didymus), one of the Twelve, was not with the disciples when Jesus came. So the other disciples told him, 'We have seen the Lord!' But he said to them, 'Unless I see the nail marks in his hands and put my finger where the nails were, and put my hand into his side, I will not believe.' A week later his disciples were in the house again, and Thomas was with them. Though the doors were locked, Jesus came and stood among them and said, 'Peace be with you!' Then he said to Thomas, 'Put your finger here; see my hands. Reach out your hand and put it into my side. Stop doubting and believe.' Thomas said to him, 'My Lord and my God!' Then Jesus told him, 'Because you have seen me, you have believed; blessed are those who have not seen and yet have believed.'"

- John 20:24-29

JAMES
THE LESS

BROTHER OF MATTHEW, AND PERHAPS SON
OF MARY, WIFE OF CLEOPHAS (AKA
ALPHAEUS)

JAMES THE LESS EVANGELIZED SYRIA AND
LED THE CHURCH THERE

LATER STONED IN JERUSALEM AFTER
REFUSING TO DENY HIS LORD

Rap Sheet

James the Less

James the Less remains one of the most obscure apostles in the Bible. We know that he is the son of Alphaeus (Luke 6:15). His mother's name is Mary (Mark 15:40), and he has a brother named Joseph (Matthew 27:56). Besides these scant details about his family, Scripture provides little more information about him. This might be one of the reasons he is referred to as James the Less. However, it's crucial for us to remember that despite his somewhat background role, James the Less was selected by Christ to be one of the twelve Apostles tasked with spreading the Gospel to the world. Jesus personally trained and utilized him in impactful ways to advance the Gospel message. James the Less was chosen because he was a valuable member of an elite team of evangelists.

Among these Twelve Ordinary Men, the life of James the Less suggests that his obscurity might have been the defining characteristic of his life. It's entirely possible that James the Less' complete anonymity reveals something profound about his character: that you don't have to be flamboyant or outspoken to achieve success.

The Apostle James, son of Alphaeus, was also known as James the Less or James the Lesser. This distinction was used to differentiate him from James, the son of Zebedee and the brother of the Apostle John. Additionally, there's a third James mentioned in the New Testament scriptures. He was the brother of Jesus, a leader in the Jerusalem church, and the author of the Book of James.

The Apostle Matthew, also called Levi the tax collector, is identified in Mark 2:14 as the son of Alphaeus. However, most scholars doubt that he and James the Lesser were related.

The title "James the Lesser" or "the Little" is used to differentiate him from the Apostle James, son of Zebedee, who was a part of Jesus' inner circle and the first disciple to be martyred.

Some scholars still debate whether James the Lesser was the disciple who first saw the risen Christ in 1 Corinthians

15:7: *"Then he appeared to James, then to all the apostles."* (ESV)

What we do know is that James the Less was personally chosen by Jesus to be a disciple and later appointed as an apostle. He might have been the first disciple to witness the risen Savior, as mentioned in 1 Corinthians 15:7. He was present with the other eleven apostles in the upper room in Jerusalem after Christ's ascension to heaven.

While his accomplishments may remain unknown to us today, James the Less might have been overshadowed by the more prominent apostles. However, the fact remains that being named among the twelve was no small achievement.

Although James the Less is one of the least known of the 12 Apostles, we cannot overlook the fact that each of these men sacrificed everything to follow Christ. Consider the words of their spokesperson Peter, who once said, *"We have left all we had to follow you!"* (Luke 18:28 NIV) Indeed, the disciples gave up their families, friends, homes, jobs, and everything familiar to them in order to follow Christ.

For all we know, "Little James" could have been an unsung hero of faith. Evidently, he did not seek recognition or fame, as he received no glory or credit for his service to Christ.

Perhaps the lesson we can derive from the obscure life of James the Less is reflected in this Psalm: *"Not to us, O Lord, not to us, but to your name give glory..."* (Psalm 115:1, ESV)

According to tradition, he was crucified in Sinai or possibly stoned to death in Jerusalem.

SIMON
THE ZEALOT

LEFT JERUSALEM TO EVANGELIZE EGYPT,
NORTH AFRICA, CARTHAGE

FROM CARTHAGE HE MOVED ON TO SPAIN AND
BRITAIN

TWO STRONG TRADITIONS OF HIS DEATH:
SAWN IN TWO IN PERSIA OR CRUCIFIED IN
BRITAIN 61 AD

Rap Sheet

Simon the Zealot

History indicates that Simon, in his younger days, was likely a political activist. Despite his lifestyle and background, it's astonishing that Jesus would choose someone like Simon to be an apostle. Perhaps Jesus recognized his fierce loyalties, incredible passion, courage, and zeal. Simon had embraced the truth and accepted Christ as his Lord. The same fervent enthusiasm he once directed towards Israel was now channeled into his devotion to Christ.

Simon was known as the Zealot, which wasn't merely a profession but a political stance. He was also referred to as a Canaanite. The Zealots were involved in politics and anarchy, aiming to overthrow the Roman government. Simon might have been a politician or a revolutionary. Upon joining Jesus, he maintained his zeal, but now it was directed towards Jesus and not any personal political ambitions.

While the exact details aren't known, tradition suggests that after preaching on the west coast of Africa, Simon traveled to England where he was crucified in 74 AD.

JUDAS
OR
THADDEUS
SON OF JAMES

AKA JUDE, JUDAS THADDAEUS, LEBBAEUS, OR
THADDAEUS

FIRST APOSTLE TO LEAVE JERUSALEM FOR
MISSIONS AND FIRST TO PREACH TO A FOREIGN
KING

BEGAN THE WORK IN ARMENIA 43-66 AD.
LATER HELPER BOTH BARTHOLOMEW AND
THOMAS

MARTYRED AND BURIED IN NEARBY IRAN

Rap Sheet

Judas or Thaddeus

Not much is known about the Apostle Judas; he lived in obscurity as one of the Twelve disciples. He is mentioned in scripture where he asked Jesus a question in John 14:22. He said, "Lord, why are you revealing yourself only to us and not to the world at large?" Christ responded and said, "He would reveal Himself to anyone who loved Him. 'If a man loves me, he will keep my words: and my Father will love him, and we will come unto him, and make our abode with him.'"

In the book called "Twelve Ordinary Men" by John MacArthur, which focuses on the apostles, Thaddeus is characterized as a tender-hearted, gentle man who displayed childlike humility.

According to most early traditions, a few years after Pentecost, Judas, the son of James, took the gospel north to Edessa, where he healed the King of Edessa, Abgar. Eusebius, the historian, mentioned that the archives at Edessa once held records of Judas' visit and the healing of Abgar; however, these records have now been destroyed.

The traditional symbol for Judas is a club, as tradition says he was clubbed to death for his faith.

JUDAS ISCARIOT

BETRAYED WITH A KISS

Rap Sheet

Judas Iscariot

Judas (detail) from The Last Supper by Carl Bloch

Judas Iscariot, the betrayer, was the son of Simon Iscariot. During the discourse in the upper room, Jesus addressed the disciples with these words: *"Did I not choose you, the twelve? Yet one of you is a devil." This was in reference to Judas, the son of Simon Iscariot, who was one of the twelve and would later betray Him* (John 6:70-71). Despite this mention, very little is known about Judas' background, and his encounter and call by Jesus are not recorded in Scripture. It is known, however, that he was not from Galilee. He spent three years with Jesus, offering his time but not his heart.

Judas infamously betrayed Jesus with a kiss in exchange for thirty pieces of silver (Matthew 26:15).

"The other eleven apostles serve as great sources of encouragement, showing us that even ordinary individuals with common flaws can be employed by God in extraordinary and remarkable ways. Judas' actions, on the other hand, stand as a cautionary tale about the potential evil that can arise from spiritual negligence, wasted opportunities, and sinful desires, which ultimately lead to a hardened heart. Here, we observe a man who achieved the closest human proximity to Jesus possible. He enjoyed every privilege granted by Christ, personally learning the teachings Jesus imparted. Despite all this, he persisted in unbelief.

Betrayed with a kiss!

As Jesus was speaking these words, a crowd, led by Judas, one of the twelve disciples, approached. Judas approached Jesus and greeted him with a kiss. However, Jesus responded, asking, 'Judas, would you betray the Son of Man with a kiss?'"

(Luke 22:47-48)

MATTHIAS

BEST KNOWN AS THE APOSTLES CHOICE TO
REPLACED JUDAS ISCARIOT AFTER HIS
BETRAYAL OF JESUS TO THE JEWISH COUNCIL.

Rap Sheet

Matthias

Matthias is not mentioned among Jesus' disciples or followers in the three synoptic gospels. However, according to Acts 1:21-26, he was with Jesus from His baptism by John the Baptist until His ascension. Following the ascension of Christ and the death of Judas Iscariot, Peter proposed to the gathering of about 120 disciples that they select two individuals to choose from, in order to fill Judas' vacant position.

Peter emphasized that the chosen individual should be someone who had been present throughout Jesus' time among them, from John's baptism to His ascension. This was because such a person would be a credible witness to Jesus' resurrection. Two men were nominated: Joseph, also known as Barsabbas or Justus, and Matthias. After praying and seeking the Lord's guidance, they cast lots, which resulted in Matthias being chosen to join the eleven apostles.

After forty days, Jesus instructed them to go beyond Judea and spread the message of God's work to the world. He then instructed them to remain in Jerusalem for an additional ten days to receive a special anointing. On that day, when the disciples had gathered together, the Holy Spirit descended upon everyone in the room.

While there is limited information about Matthias, it's important to note that he was present throughout Jesus' ministry, from His baptism by John the Baptist to His Resurrection and Ascension. As a firsthand witness to these significant events, Matthias met the qualifications to be considered an Apostle.

It is widely believed that Matthias carried out his ministry in Judaea before embarking on missions to foreign lands. According to Greek tradition, he brought the gospel to Cappadocia, a mountainous region now situated in central Turkey. Later, he is said to have journeyed to the region near the Caspian Sea, where he met his martyrdom, either through crucifixion or, according to some accounts, by being dismembered.

PAUL

Even though Paul was not one of the original Apostles, Jesus called him to the ministry on the road to Damascus. The story of Paul's conversion is told in Acts 9:1-19 and retold by Paul in Acts 22:6-21 and Acts 26:12-18. Paul became one of the most important men in the ministry.

Paul wrote more epistles than any other Apostle

Beheaded by Nero

Rap Sheet

Paul

Paul, originally known by his birth name Saul, was born into a Jewish family in the city of Tarsus. Tarsus held the status of a Roman "free city," granting him Roman citizenship, a privilege he would later exercise in his life.

Saul's early religious education was received at the renowned Rabbi school in Jerusalem, where he was taught under the guidance of the well-known and respected Pharisee, Gamaliel.

At the age of thirty, as a Pharisee, Saul played an official role as a witness during the stoning of Stephen. His fervour for what he perceived as God's law and his commitment to halting the early propagation of Christianity knew no bounds.

Witnessing Stephen's stoning only intensified Saul's zeal to spearhead the wave of persecution against the flourishing Christian community.

When Paul later contemplated his days before his conversion, he reflected, *"For you have heard of my former conduct in Judaism, how I persecuted the church of God beyond measure and tried to destroy it. And I advanced in Judaism beyond many of my contemporaries in my own nation, being more exceedingly zealous for the traditions of my fathers."* (Galatians 1:13-14, HBFV)

His relentless dedication to eradicating followers of Jesus' teachings propelled him to commit even more audacious acts, including searching from house to house to locate believers in Jesus (Acts 8:1, 3). In his unyielding efforts to curb the dissemination of these nascent Christian beliefs in Jerusalem, his zeal spurred him to root out any traces of Christian influence within synagogues, not only in Jerusalem but also in other regions. With that goal in mind, he pursued and obtained written permission from the temple's High Priest to eradicate any influence of this new ideology from the synagogues in the surrounding city. His aim was to apprehend those who believed in Jesus as the Messiah and escort them to Jerusalem for punishment.

The most pivotal event in Paul's life occurred during his journey to Damascus. The Bible recounts a heavenly spotlight shining upon him and his companions as they travelled, while the voice of Jesus asked, *"Saul, Saul, why do you persecute Me?"* (Acts 9:4) As a result of this supernatural encounter, God took away his sight, and his companions had to guide him into the city. This Damascus experience led to his complete repentance and eventual healing of his blindness. The culmination of this encounter facilitated Saul's baptism and reception of the Holy Spirit.

Following Saul's conversion, the same fervor and singular dedication he once directed against Christianity transformed into an intense quest to propagate the gospel throughout the known world. This transformed man is now known as Paul. His remarkable ministry spanned thirty-five years until his passing at the age of sixty-six.

Key moments and achievements in Paul's life include his witnessing of Stephen's stoning. After his encounter on the road to Damascus, his period of blindness and subsequent healing, Jesus personally instructed him for three years while he resided in Arabia.

During his ministry, he was endowed with the power to raise the dead, and he himself was resurrected after being stoned to the point of death in Lystra. *"A group of Jews from Antioch and Iconium came to Lystra and won over the crowds. Then they stoned Paul and dragged him out of the city, assuming he was dead. However, as the disciples gathered around him, he stood up, reentered the city, and the next day departed for Derbe."* (Acts 14:19)

Paul undertook at least five evangelistic journeys, visiting over 50 cities during his travels. He even preached the gospel to Emperor Caesar and his entire household.

Additionally, he authored at least fourteen books or epistles in the Bible, mentored other evangelists and gospel preachers—including John Mark and Timothy—despite enduring over five years in prison.

Although scripture doesn't provide an account of Paul's death, it is one of the more extensively documented martyrdoms in the early church. Numerous early church fathers wrote that he was beheaded by Emperor Nero, which would place his death before 68 AD.

The letter is from Paul, an apostle. I wasn't appointed by any group of people or human authority, but by Jesus Christ himself and by God the Father, who raised Jesus from the dead. (Galatians 1:1)

Defining Statement

These ordinary men, through the power of the Holy Spirit, did extraordinary things for God and set the example for us today. They formed the foundation of the Christian church, initiating a movement that is still steadily spreading across the face of the earth. We are part of that movement today.

SUMMING UP THE APOSTLES

The apostles were a team in every sense of the word. Despite their distinct personalities, diverse backgrounds, and varying gifts, Jesus ingrained in them the understanding that for the gospel to have a greater impact, they must collaborate as a team. Their unity wasn't for self-promotion but for the sake of the Kingdom.

SEVENTY-TWO DISCIPLES

The Lord selected seventy-two disciples and dispatched them in pairs ahead to the towns and places he intended to visit. His instructions to them were as follows:

"The harvest is plentiful, but the workers are few. Therefore, pray to the Lord in charge of the harvest, asking him to send more workers into his fields. Now, go, and bear in mind that I am sending you out like lambs among wolves. Do not carry money or a traveler's bag, nor an extra pair of sandals. Also, refrain from stopping to greet anyone on the road.

(Luke 10:1-4) NIV

Recall that a disciple is a student, and an Apostle is someone who has been sent. In my view, after Christ's ascension, it's a natural progression that all the existing disciples were elevated to the status of Apostles.

Upon ascending into heaven, Jesus left these words with His disciples:

"Go ye therefore, and teach all nations, baptizing them in the name of the Father, and of the Son, and of the Holy Ghost: Teaching them to observe all things whatsoever I have commanded you: and, lo, I am with you always, even unto the end of the world. Amen."

(Matthew 28:19-20)

Partial Lists of the Apostles' Names, and Their Station Assignment in Ministry

Attributed To Hippolytus

JAMES	CLEOPAS	MATTHIAS
The Lord's brother, Bishop of Jerusalem	Bishop of Jerusalem	Who supplied the vacant place in the number of the twelve apostles
THADDEUS	ANANIAS	STEPHEN
Who conveyed the epistle to Augarus (Abgar V)	Who baptized Paul, and was bishop of Damascus	The first martyr
PHILIP	PROCHORUS	NICANOR
Who baptized the Ethiopian eunuch	Bishop of Nicomedia, who also was the first that departed, 11 believing together with his daughters	Died when Stephen was martyred

TIMON Bishop of Bostra	**PARMENAS** Bishop of Soli	**NICOLAUS** Bishop of Samaria
BARNABAS Bishop of Milan	**MARK THE EVANGELIST*** Bishop of Alexandria	**LUKE THE EVANGELIST***
SILAS Bishop of Corinth	**SILVANUS** Bishop of Thessalonica	**CRISCES (CRESCENS)** Bishop of Carchedon in Gaul
EPÆNETUS Bishop of Carthage	**ANDRONICUS** Bishop of Pannonia	**STACHYS** Bishop of Byzantium
AMPLIAS Bishop of Odyssus	**PHYGELLUS** Bishop of Ephesus. He was of the party of Simon	**HERMOGENES** He, too, was of the same mind with the former
BARNABAS Bishop of Heraclea	**URBAN** Bishop of Macedonia	**ARISTOBULUS** Bishop of Britain
DEMAS	**APELLES**	**AGABUS**

Who also became a priest of idols	Bishop of Smyrna	The prophet
NARCISSUS Bishop of Athens	**HERODION** Bishop of Tarsus	**PHLEGON** Bishop of Marathon
RUFUS Bishop of Thebes	**ASYNCRITUS** Bishop of Hyrcania	**HERMAS** Bishop of Philippopolis (Thrace)
HERMES Bishop of Dalmatia	**PATROBULUS** Bishop of Puteoli	**PHILOLOGUS** Bishop of Sinope
LINUS Bishop of Rome	**CAIUS** Bishop of Ephesus	**LUCIUS** Bishop of Laodicea in Syria
OLYMPUS Martyred in Rome	**RHODION** Martyred in Rome	**TERTIUS** Bishop of Iconium
JASON Bishop of Tarsus	**SOSIPATER** Bishop of Iconium	**APOLLOS** Bishop of Cæsarea
ERASTUS Bishop of Panellas	**QUARTUS** Bishop of Berytus	**TYCHICUS** Bishop of Colophonia
CEPHAS	**SOSTHENES**	**MARK**

	Bishop of Colophonia	Cousin to Barnabas, Bishop of Apollonia
EPAPHRODITUS Bishop of Andriace	**CÆSAR** Bishop of Dyrrachium	**CLEMENT** Bishop of Sardinia
JUSTUS Bishop of Eleutheropolis	**ARTEMAS** Bishop of Lystra	**CARPUS** Bishop of Berytus in Thrace
ONESIPHORUS Bishop of Corone	**TYCHICUS** Bishop of Chalcedon	**MARK** Who is also John, Bishop of Bibloupolis
EVODUS Bishop of Antioch	**ARISTARCHUS** Bishop of Apamea	**ZENAS** Bishop of Diospolis
PHILEMON Bishop of Gaza	**PUDES**	**TROPHIMUS** Who was martyred along with Paul

*These two [Mark and Luke] belonged to the seventy disciples who were scattered by the offence of the word which Christ spoke, *"Except a man eat my flesh, and drink my blood, he is not worthy of me."*

What Ever Happened To These Guys?

The New Testament tells of the fate of only two of the apostles: Judas, who betrayed Jesus and then went out and hanged himself, and James the son of Zebedee, who was executed by Herod about 44 A D (Acts 12:2).

PETER - Demise: Crucified Upside Down: Died 33-34 years after the death of Christ. He and Paul were the founders of the church at Rome and recognized as the head of the original Christian community in Jerusalem. He left the city when King Herod Agrippa I started to persecute Christians in Jerusalem and ordered the beheading of the (the Great). After escaping from Jerusalem, Peter preached in Judea and in Antioch where he is historically considered the first bishop of the Orthodox Church. Peter went back to Rome and converted thousands into Christianity. During the persecution under Nero about 66 A. D, **Peter was crucified upside-down at his own request, because he felt that he wasn't worthy of being crucified the same way as our Lord.**

ANDREW - Demise: Crucified Upside Down on an X-shaped cross: Went to the "land of the man-eaters," in what is now the Soviet Union. Christians there claim him as the first to bring the gospel to their land. He also preached in Asia Minor, modern-day Turkey, and in Greece, where he is said to have been crucified there. Preached in Georgia (Russia), Istanbul (Turkey), Macedonia and finally Greece. In Patros, Greece, the Governor Aegiatis was angered by the apostle's preaching and the conversion of his own family to Christianity. After refusing to renounce his faith, **the governor ordered that Andrew be crucified, bound to a X shape cross not nailed.** As he was dying, he kept preaching, he convinced many to accept Christianity, he died after suffering for three days.

JAMES (the Greater) - Demise: He was Beheaded: The son of Zebedee, the brother of the. Was the first apostle to be martyred for his faith. One of the only two apostles (Judas Iscariot) to have their martyrdom recorded in Scripture. He was captured and condemned to die by Herod & Agrippa, to please Jewish leaders. **He was beheaded shortly before the day of the Passover in the year 44AD** or about 11 years after the death of Christ (Acts 12: 1-2)

JOHN (the Beloved)- Demise: Thrown into Boiling Oil, but Survived: Took care of Mary the mother of Jesus in his home. Was the leader of the church in the Ephesus. Is the only Apostle thought to have died a natural death from old age. John escaped persecution of Herod Agrippa I and preached for some time in Asia Minor. Later, he went back to Rome, where he was persecuted and thrown into a cauldron of boiling oil, but miraculously he survived. Then emperor Domitian had him banished to the island of Patmos. When Domitian died, John went back to Ephesus, where he spent the rest of his days. **He died a very old man at the age of 88.**

MATTHEW - Demise: Stabbed to Death? Ministered in Persia and Ethiopia. Had a long life because the Gospel of Matthew was written at least twenty years after the death of Christ. Christian tradition says he preached in Ethiopia, Judea, Macedonia, Syria, and Parthia. **Martyred by being stabbed to death in Ethiopia, killed with a spear with an ax attached in the city of Nadabah, Ethiopia around A.D. 60.** Bible scholars have different versions on how he died. **Some say he was either killed with a sword in Parthia or he died a natural death in Ethiopia.**

PHILIP - Demise: Crucified Upside Down: Possibly had a powerful ministry in Carthage in North Africa and then in Asia Minor. Philip partnered with Bartholomew and preached in Greece, Syria and in Turkey in the cities of Galatia, Phrygia and Hierapolis. Through his miraculous healing and preaching, Philip converted the wife of the proconsul of the city of Hierapolis. This angered the proconsul who ordered that both Philip and Bartholomew be tortured and **crucified upside down, impaled by iron hooks in his ankles and hung upside down to die, preaching to death 54 AD in Heliopolis, Egypt.** While dying, Philip continued to preach and convinced the crowd and the proconsul to release Bartholomew, but Philip died that day.

THADDAEUS or JUDAS - Demise: Sawed or Axed to Death? The traditional symbol Thaddeus is a club because tradition says he was clubbed to death for his faith. He partnered with Simon, the Zealot, they preached and converted non-believers in Judea (Israel), Persia (Iran), Samaria (Israel), Idumaea (near Jordan), Syria, Mesopotamia (Iran) and Libya. It is believed that Thaddeus travelled and preached in Beirut, Lebanon. Helped Bartholomew bringing Christianity to Armenia. **He was either crucified in Edessa, Turkey; or he was clubbed-to-death and his**

body was sawed or axed in pieces together with Simon the Zealot. He was buried either in Northern Persia or at St. Peter's Basilica in Rome.

THOMAS - Demise: Impaled by a Spear: Readily known as "Doubting Thomas" for disbelieving the Lord's Resurrection. But after his doubts were erased, he became a fearless preacher of the Gospel. Was most active in east of Syria. Tradition has him preaching as far east as India, where Christians revere him as their founder. **They claim that he died there when pierced through with the spears by four soldiers.** He was one of the first Apostles to preach outside of the Roman Empire. He preached in Babylon (present day Iraq) and established its first Christian church. He went to Persia (Iran) and travelled as far as China and India. He was martyred in Mylapore, India when a local king named Masdai condemned him to death. The Brahmins (high ranked priests/scholars who served as the king's advisers) thought Christianity disrespected India's Caste System. **Thomas was brought to a nearby mountain and was stabbed to death with a spear.**

BARTHOLOMEW or NATHANAEL - Demise: Skinned Alive and Beheaded: By tradition had widespread missionary travels attributed to him, to India with Thomas, back to Armenia, and also to Ethiopia and Southern Arabia. There are various accounts of how he met his death as a martyr for the gospel. Nathanael died as a martyr while serving the people of Albinopolis, Armenia. was martyred, most likely he was flayed (skin peeled from his body) and then beheaded. Preached the Gospel in Mesopotamia, Persia, Turkey, Armenia and India. **He was skinned alive (flayed) and beheaded at Derbent Azerbaijan,** by order of a local king after a majority of the people of Derbent converted to Christianity.

JAMES (the Lesser) the son of Alpheus - Demise: Stoned and Clubbed to Death: As reported by Jewish historian Josephus. We know he lived at least five years after the death of Christ because of mentions in the Bible. Preached in Damascus and acknowledged as the first bishop of the Christians in Jerusalem. He was sentenced to be stoned-to-death for challenging Jewish Laws and for convincing some members of the Jewish community to convert to Christianity. There are two accounts of his death. 1) He was stoned and beaten with a fuller's club or 2) he was thrown from the pinnacle of the temple but survived, then he was beaten to death with a fuller's club. Records indicate that he was buried on the spot where he died.

SIMON THE ZEALOT - Demise: Sawed or Axed to Death? Ministered in Persia and was killed after refusing to sacrifice to the sun god. Before becoming an, was a member of the "Zealots", a political movement rebelling against the Roman occupation. Identified by some as the second Bishop of Jerusalem after James the Lesser (who was beheaded). Preached in the Middle East, North Africa, Egypt, Mauritania and even Britain. His martyrdom may have been; **crucified by the Romans in Lincolnshire, Britain, or crucified in Samaria** (Israel) after a failed revolt or sawed-to-death in Suanir, Persia with Thaddeus.

JUDAS ISCARIOT - Demise: Suicide, Death by Hanging He hung himself after he betrayed Jesus. Best known as the betrayed the Lord by divulging His location, leading to His arrest and persecution. He received 30 pieces of silver from Jewish priests for the information he gave. **Shortly after the death of Christ, Judas hung himself,** (Matthew 27:5) at Aceldama.

MATTHIAS - Demise: Crucifixion: Was the apostle chosen to replace Judas Iscariot. Preached in Syria with Andrew and Later he journeyed to the region near the Caspian Sea, where **he was martyred crucifixion and, according to others he was, chopped apart.**

PAUL - Demise: Beheaded Commissioned as an apostle by Jesus himself on the road to Damascus. Martyred in Rome about 66 A D, during the persecution of the Jews under Emperor Nero. **Paul was tortured and then beheaded because Roman citizens could not be crucified.**

Final Summary of the Twelve Apostles

Jesus Christ selected twelve men from among his early followers to become his closest spiritual companions. They had no extraordinary skills. Neither religious, nor were they refined, they were ordinary people, just like you and me. They would have been considered common men in their day.

We find the names of the twelve apostles in Matthew 10:2-4 Mark 3:14-19 Luke 6:13-16:

"And when day came, he called his disciples and chose from them twelve, whom he named apostles: Simon, whom he named Peter, and Andrew his brother, and James and John, and Philip, and Bartholomew, and Matthew, and Thomas, and James the son of Alphaeus, and Simon who was called the Zealot, and Judas the son of James, and Judas Iscariot, who became a traitor"(ESV).

The replacement for Judas Iscariot (ACTS 1:26)

And they gave forth their lots; and the lot fell upon Matthias; and he was numbered with the eleven apostles.

These men became the pioneering leaders of the New Testament church, but they were not without faults and shortcomings. **Interestingly, not one of the chosen twelve disciples was a scholar or rabbi.**

Jesus taught them about the kingdom of heaven, and in return he learned much from them about the kingdom of men.

These twelve men represented many different types of human temperament.

In a religious sense, they were laymen, unlearned in the lore of the rabbis and untrained in the methods of rabbinical interpretation of the Scriptures.

God chose them for a purpose—to fan the flames of the gospel that would spread across the face of the earth and continue to burn bright throughout the centuries to follow, even to this very day.

He selected and used each of these regular men to carry out his exceptional plan. Their love and loyalty to Jesus made them uncommon heroes.

After an intensive three-year discipleship training course with Jesus, and following his resurrection from the dead, the Lord fully commissioned the apostles to advance God's kingdom and carry the gospel message to the world.

Then the eleven disciples went away into Galilee, into a mountain where Jesus had appointed them. And when they saw him, they worshipped him: but some doubted. And Jesus came and spake unto them, saying, All power is given unto me in heaven and in earth.

Go ye therefore, and teach all nations, baptizing them in the name of the Father, and of the Son, and of the Holy Ghost: Teaching them to observe all things whatsoever I have commanded you: and, lo, I am with you always, even unto the end of the world.

(Matthew 28:16-20)

So then after the Lord had spoken unto them, he was received up into heaven, and sat on the right hand of God. And they went forth, and preached everywhere, the Lord working with them, and confirming the word with signs following.

(Mark 16:19-20)

Take a few moments now to review what we have discovered about the apostles, who helped ignite the light of truth that still dwells within us today and calls us to come and follow the man called Jesus Christ.

Andrew

- Brother of Peter.
- Was the first chosen disciple of Christ.
-Considered the "director general" of the disciple corps.
- Actively brought others to Christ.
- Served as chairman of the apostolic corps.
- Was 33 years old when he joined Jesus, making him the oldest of the disciples.
- Recognized as a proficient organizer and efficient administrator.
- Known for his good judgment of character.
- Met his demise being crucified on the cross.

Simon Peter

- Brother of Andrew.
- Along with James and John, part of Christ's inner circle.
- Appointed by Jesus as his personal assistant to cater to his physical needs and miscellaneous tasks.
- Chosen to accompany Jesus during his long night vigils of prayer and

communion with God.

- Jesus had known Simon before Andrew introduced him as the second disciple.

- Peter was 30 years old when Jesus called him to be a disciple.

- Peter was married and had three children.

- Jesus was familiar with Peter even before he met Andrew.

- Peter was known for being erratic and impulsive.

- Often spoke his mind, leading to conflicts with others.

- Frequently asked Jesus questions. While most were valid, some were considered thoughtless or foolish.

- Peter was an accomplished preacher.

- He made significant contributions to the kingdom, second only to Paul among the disciples.

James Zebedee

- James was the older brother of John.

- Along with Peter and John, James became a personal assistant to Christ.

- They attended to Jesus' physical and personal needs.

- Chosen to accompany Jesus on his long nights of prayer.

- James was 30 years old when chosen as a disciple by Jesus.

- He was married and had four children.

- Known for his quick temper.

- Recognized as a thoughtful thinker and planner.

James, along with a few others, was among the best public preachers of the group.

He was the first disciple to be martyred.

Known as James "the Greater" to distinguish him from the disciple James "the Less".

John Zebedee

- John, along with Peter and James, was a personal companion of Christ.
- Shared the same duties and responsibilities as Peter and James.
- John was 24 years old when Jesus called him to be a disciple.

- He was the youngest of the disciples and was not married at the time.

- Prone to losing his temper but generally was a man of few words.

- Possessed a creative imagination.

- John Zebedee is believed to be the only disciple to die of natural causes.

- He passed away around A.D. 103 at the age of 101.

Matthew

- Often referred to as Levi, Matthew was the group's bookkeeper.
- He was responsible for maintaining financial records.
- When ministry funds or donations were insufficient, Matthew would inform the twelve disciples and direct them back to their previous professions (like fishing) until the treasury was replenished.
- Matthew was the seventh disciple chosen by Jesus.
- He was 31 years old, married, and had four children.
- Recognized as a profound businessman.
- Known for his friendly nature and ability to easily forge friendships.
- Generously contributed most of his savings to the ministry.

Philip

- Served as the steward of the group.
- His duty included ensuring food provisions and attending to the needs of visitors and, at times, feeding the multitudes of listeners.
- At the age of 27, he was chosen by Jesus as the fifth disciple.

- He was newly married and had no children.

- He was one among three boys and four girls in his family.

- Possessed a straightforward mindset and lacked imagination.

- While not expected to achieve monumental tasks, he excelled at executing small tasks with great dedication.

- He was an average public speaker but proved to be persuasive and an effective worker.

Thaddaeus

- Along with James "the Less", Thaddaeus was responsible for crowd control.

- Their duty was to identify and deputize enough followers to maintain order during Jesus's preachings.

- Thaddaeus worked as a fisherman by trade.

- He was married and had at least one child.

- Together with Philip, he managed food and supplies for the group.

- Assisted in distributing money to families in need.

- Was also referred to as Jude, Lebbaeus, and Judas.

Thomas a.k.a. Didymus

- Managed the planned places to visit.
- Responsible for arranging accommodations and helping select locations for teaching and preaching.
- He was the eighth disciple chosen and was introduced to Jesus by Philip.
- Became a disciple at the age of 29.

- Married and had four children.
- Initially worked as a carpenter and stone mason but later earned a living as a fisherman.
- Possessed a logical and sharp mind despite limited formal education.
- Had a tendency to be disagreeable and quarrelsome.
- Excelled as a businessman but struggled with mood swings.
- Recognized by Jesus for his genuine dedication due to his strong work ethic.

Bartholomew

- Managed the needs of the disciples' families, receiving reports and arranging funds to assist them.
- Brought to Jesus by his friend Philip.
- Became a disciple at the age of 25.
- Youngest in a family of seven.
- Unmarried and the sole support for his elderly parents.
- Recognized as the apostolic philosopher and dreamer of the group.
- One of the best-educated men among the twelve.
- Also known as Nathaniel.

James "the Less"

- Along with Judas, James was responsible for crowd control during Jesus's preaching.
- James worked as a fisherman by trade.
- Called to discipleship at the age of 26.
- Married with three children.
- Thought to be the cousin of Jesus.
- Assisted Philip with supplies.
- Aided Nathaniel in caring for the families of the disciples.
- Known as James the Lesser to distinguish from James Zebedee.

Simon (the Zealot)

- In charge of recreation for the group, responsible for finding times and ways to relax.
- He was the eleventh disciple, brought to Jesus by Simon-Peter.
- Chosen as a disciple at the age of 28.
- Known for speaking without thinking.
- Highly efficient as an organizer.
- A skilled debater.

Judas Iscariot

- Judas was the treasurer for the group, responsible for the money bag, bookkeeping, bill payments, and budget.
- He was the only son of wealthy Jewish parents.
- Joined the disciples at the age of 30.
- Unmarried.
- The only Judean among the twelve.
- Skilled in business and executive matters.
- A strict and effective organizer.
- Struggled with handling losses.
- Highly educated.

Matthias

- Elected from among the 120 disciples to replace Judas Iscariot as the twelfth apostle.
- Received the Holy Spirit along with the other apostles on the day of Pentecost.
- Preached the gospel in Judea and Colchis.
- Ultimately met his demise by crucifixion.

Paul

- Personally commissioned by Jesus Himself.
- Converted on the road to Damascus.
- Personally taught and prepared for ministry by Jesus for three years.
- Present at the stoning of Stephen, the first Christian martyr.
- Credited with writing 13 books of the Bible.
- Held Roman citizenship.

The above apostle information (except for James "the Less", Matthias, Paul and Judas Thaddaeus) was cited from the following sources:

http://truthbook.com/jesus/the-twelve-apostles
http://christianity.about.com/od/peopleofthebible/tp/12-Apostles.htm

Truthbook.com denoted James "the Less" and Judas Thaddaeus as being twins.

(Acts 1:13) clearly denotes Judas as the brother of James, therefore, independent online researches (other than truthbook.com) was performed on these two apostles.

WAIVER of TRUTH:

All information comprised in this document (including the individual apostle documents) are not to be considered as being 100% accurate; however; all research work was performed with due diligence to be as accurate as possible

How They Died
Based on the Bible information or Tradition

Peter
Crucified upside Down
66 AD

Matthew
Stabbed or Beheaded
60 AD

Andrew
Crucified on an
X-shaped Cross
60 AD

Thomas
Pierced With
A Spear - 72 AD

James (The Beloved)
Beheaded
44 AD

James (The Less)
Clubbed To Death
66 AD

John
Died of old age
He was 88 years old
99AD

Simon (the Zealot)
Sawn in Half or crucified
74 AD

Philip
Crucified up side down
54 AD

Jude
Clubbed to Death
Or Beheaded - 65 AD

Bartholomew
Skinned Alive (Flayed)
and Beheaded
68 AD

Judas Iscariot
Suicide
30 AD

Matthias
Stabbed or Beheaded
64 AD

Paul
Crucified
Between 64-66 AD

Old Testament Authors

Traditionally, both Jews and Christians believe Moses is the author and compiler of Genesis and each of the first five books of the Bible also called the Pentateuch:

- **Genesis**- Moses
- **Exodus**- Moses
- **Leviticus**- Moses
- **Numbers**- Moses
- **Deuteronomy**- Moses

These are the five Books of the Law:

- *Genesis,* meaning "beginning" since it recounts the beginning of God's creation.
- *Exodus,* which means "exit" or "departure," referring to the journey of the Hebrews from out of slavery in Egypt;
- *Leviticus,* a book detailing worship as led by the priests ordained from the tribe of Levi;
- *Numbers,* whose title is derived from the book's opening account of the census or numbering of the people of Israel;
- *Deuteronomy,* meaning "second law," since it

gives a detailed listing of the additional laws given by God through Moses.

This second group of the Old Testament is known as the historical books.

- **Joshua**- Unknown
- **Judges**- Unknown
- **Ruth**- Unknown
- **1 & 2 Samuel**- Unknown
- **1 & 2 Kings**- Unknown
- **1 & 2 Chronicles**- Ezra
- **Ezra**- Ezra
- **Nehemiah**- Nehemiah
- **Esther**- Unknown

This third group of the Old Testament are the books of Wisdom,_proclaiming that happiness is possible only through faith in and obedience to the one true God.

- **Job**- Unknown
- **Psalms**- Various authors: David is credited for 73 of the Psalms, Asaph is credited for 12, Sons of Korah for 11, Solomon for 2, Moses, Ethan, and Heman for one each, and 50 are unknown.

- **Proverbs**- Various authors: Solomon is credited for 29 of the Proverbs, Agar and Lemuel for one each.
- **Ecclesiastes**- Solomon
- **Song of Solomon**- Solomon

The fourth and final section of the Old Testament includes the books of prophecy. These serve as an introduction to John the Baptist's preparation of the world for the coming of the Messiah, who is Isaiah's Suffering Servant, Zechariah's Prince of Peace, and the Good Shepherd lays down His life for the flock.

- **Isaiah**- Isaiah
- **Jeremiah**- Jeremiah
- **Lamentations**- Jeremiah
- **Ezekiel**- Ezekiel
- **Daniel**- Daniel
- **Hosea**- Hosea
- **Joel**- Joel
- **Amos**- Amos
- **Obadiah**- Obadiah
- **Jonah**- Jonah
- **Micah**- Micah

- **Nahum**- Nahum

- **Habakkuk**- Habakkuk

- **Zephaniah**- Zephaniah

- **Haggai**- Haggai

- **Zechariah**- Zechariah

- **Malachi**-Malachi

New Testament Authors

- **Matthew**- Apostle Matthew
- **Mark**- Apostle Mark
- **Luke**- Apostle Luke
- **John**- Apostle John
- **Acts**- Apostle Luke

Paul the Apostle is credited for 13 of the Epistle books in the New Testament:

- **Romans**- Apostle Paul
- **1 Corinthians**- Apostle Paul
- **2 Corinthians**- Apostle Paul
- **Galatians**- Apostle Paul
- **Ephesians**- Apostle Paul
- **Philippians**- Apostle Paul
- **Colossians**- Apostle Paul
- **1 Thessalonians**- Apostle Paul
- **2 Thessalonians**- Apostle Paul
- **1 Timothy**- Apostle Paul
- **2 Timothy**- Apostle Paul
- **Titus**- Apostle Paul

- **Philemon**- Apostle Paul
- **Hebrews** - Unknown
- **James** - James, Brother of Christ
- **1 & 2 Peter** - Apostle Peter
- **1, 2 & 3 John** - Apostle John
- **Jude** - Jude, brother of James
- **Revelation** - Apostle John

After the crucifixion of Jesus, the disciples and other followers were left disillusioned, discouraged, and afraid; many went into hiding. The person they had believed to be the Messiah was now dead, and their hope in Him as the savior of the world had been utterly crushed. They thought the only option left was to return to their homes and their former way of life.

However, after He rose from the grave, they gathered once more and boldly proclaimed that their Savior was indeed alive. Their boldness in preaching stemmed from the fact that Jesus was alive, and numerous disciples had witnessed Him (1 Cor. 15:5 & 7). Some even shared meals and fellowship with Him (John 21:12-15) (Acts 10:41). They bore witness with their own eyes that Jesus had risen from the dead.

Their lives were filled with hardship and persecution, ultimately leading to martyrdom. Their preaching held immense power and was life-changing. They could not have sustained such unwavering faith if they had believed what they were preaching was untrue. There was only one reason these men were willing to endure such terrible persecution: because they had witnessed the Messiah being crucified and then rising from the dead; they had conversed with Him, walked with Him, and believed that this truth was worth dying for.

Bonus Information

Mark: Died in Alexandria, Egypt, after being dragged by Horses through the streets until he was dead.

Luke: Was hanged in Greece as a result of his tremendous Preaching to the lost.

Barnabas: Was dragged out of the synagogue, and he was then tortured to death.

Silas: died a martyr in 65 AD, crucified during the reign of Emperor Nero.

Made in the USA
Las Vegas, NV
17 January 2024

84509036R10066